WANTED!
— FAMOUS OUTLAWS —
BLACKBEARD

A NOTORIOUS PIRATE IN THE CARIBBEAN

TIM COOKE

Gareth Stevens
PUBLISHING

Please visit our website, **www.garethstevens.com**.
For a free color catalog of all our high-quality books,
call toll-free 1-800-542-2595 or fax 1-877-542-2596.

Library of Congress Cataloging-in-Publication Data

Cooke, Tim, 1961-
 Blackbeard : a notorious pirate in the Caribbean / Tim Cooke.
    pages cm. — (Wanted! Famous outlaws)
 Includes index.
 ISBN 978-1-4824-4247-2 (pbk.)
 ISBN 978-1-4824-4248-9 (6 pack)
 ISBN 978-1-4824-4249-6 (library binding)
 1. Teach, Edward, -1718—Juvenile literature. 2. Pirates—North Carolina—Atlantic Coast—Biography—Juvenile literature.
 3. Pirates—Virginia—Atlantic Coast—Biography—Juvenile literature. 4. North Carolina—History—Colonial period,
 ca. 1600-1775—Juvenile literature. 5. Virginia—History—Colonial period, ca. 1600-1775—Juvenile literature. I. Title.
 F257.T422C66 2016
 910.4'5—dc23
 [B]

                                        2015029034

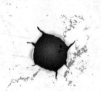

Published in 2016 by
Gareth Stevens Publishing
111 East 14th Street, Suite 349
New York, NY 10003

© 2016 Brown Bear Books Ltd

For Brown Bear Books Ltd:
Editorial Director: Lindsey Lowe
Managing Editor: Tim Cooke
Children's Publisher: Anne O'Daly
Design Manager: Keith Davis
Designer: Melissa Roskell
Picture Manager: Sophie Mortimer

Picture Credits: Front Cover: Library of Congress. ACiV Online Guidebook: 10; Alamy: Lanmas 19; Assassinscreed: 17;
Bridgeman Art Library: Look and Learn 39; Bristol Records Office: 8; Dreamstime: Alfred Wekelo 33; Dulwich Picture
Gallery: 12; Adam Faanes: 4; Governor's Palace Virginia: 29; Harper and Brothers: Howard Pyle 45; Library of Congress:
14, 16, 24, 25, 41, 44; My Photos Oracoke: 37; National Archives: 36; National Maritime Museum: 35; Prado Museum: 26;
Pyracy.com: 13; Robert Hunt Library: 20, 21, 28, 31, 40; Charles Scribner's Sons: NC Wyeth 42; Shutterstock: 5, 38, Everett
Historical 7, Olga Labusova 18, Stephen Rees 18; Thinkstock: istockphoto 15, Amanda Lewis 6; Topfoto: 43, Fine Art
Images/HIP 9, The Granger Collection 22, 23, 27, 30, The Print Collector/Heritage-Images 34.

Brown Bear Books has made every attempt to contact the copyright holders.
If anyone has any information please contact licensing@brownbearbooks.co.uk

Manufactured in the United States of America

CPSIA compliance information: Batch #CW16GS. For further information contact Gareth Stevens, New York, New York at 1-800-542-2595.

CONTENTS

INTRODUCTION

Blackbeard was one of the most feared pirates of the 18th century. He terrorized sailors along the Caribbean and North American coasts.

Blackbeard's real name was probably Edward Teach. He was thought to have been born in Bristol, England, in around 1680. Experts do not know much about Blackbeard's early life. Bristol was a port, so he may have become a sailor before turning to crime. He is first mentioned as a pirate in the Caribbean in 1716. Pirates were thieves who attacked ships at sea and stole their cargo. Sometimes they also seized the ships.

The English Royal Navy defeats the Spanish Armada, or fleet, in 1588. The victory made England the world's leading naval power.

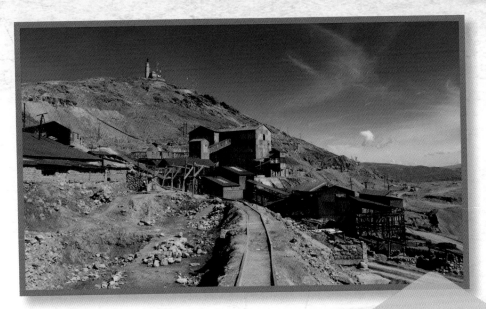

The first pirates

Pirates often operated with the official approval of their country's government. These pirates were called **privateers**. Governments wanted privateers to attack ships from other nations. They saw this as a way to weaken their enemies.

Queen Elizabeth I of England (1533–1603) asked Sir Walter Raleigh to establish a **colony** in America. She gave him permission to raid Spanish vessels and settlements. Raleigh attacked Spanish colonies in the Caribbean. The Spanish saw Raleigh as a pirate. The English saw him as a hero. Raleigh helped begin the English settlement of North America. By the 1660s English colonies stretched south along the coast from Virginia to the Carolinas.

This hill at Potosí in Bolivia was full of gold and silver. The Spanish shipped treasure from their colony in Bolivia across the Atlantic to Spain.

Privateers Sailors with official permission to raid ships from other countries.

Colony An area under the control of another country.

The success of England's new colonies was based on naval power. People in the colonies depended on ships for essential supplies. Ships also took goods produced in the colonies back home. European countries built fast, efficient ships. After the English defeated the Spanish fleet in 1588, England's Royal Navy was the most powerful naval force in Europe. As England increased its colonies in North America and the Caribbean, France and the Netherlands also tried to gain control of territory in the Caribbean islands.

Sir Walter Raleigh was a famous British privateer of the 16th century.

European jealousy

Meanwhile gold and silver from Spain's American colonies made Spain rich. The treasure had to be transported to the royal treasury in Spain. Spanish ships could not cross the Atlantic Ocean without breaking their journey to take on supplies. They stopped in the Caribbean. The Carribean was also full of ships bringing slaves from Africa to the New World.

Outlaws of the sea

As the European nations competed for control, the Caribbean became lawless. **Merchant ships** and their cargo were easy targets for other ships to attack. Many former privateers decided to become pirates. This time, they were not operating on behalf of a government. They stole in order to make money for themselves. Blackbeard was a privateer turned pirate. He quickly became the best known and most feared of all the pirates of the Caribbean.

Slaves harvest sugarcane in the Caribbean. A cargo of slaves was valuable for pirates.

Merchant ships Ships that carry cargo or passengers.

Unknown Beginnings

No one really knows much about Blackbeard's early life. Experts have tried to guess some of the details.

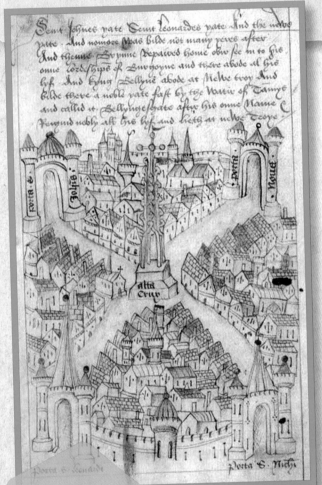

Bristol was an important English port. Ships often sailed from there across the Atlantic.

Historians believe Blackbeard was named Edward Teach. He was probably born around 1680 in the port of Bristol, England. Some people think his surname was not Teach at all, but was Thatch. Experts know that as an adult Teach could read and write. This suggests he came from a family that could afford to send him to school. In 17th-century England, wealthier families often sent their sons into the shipping trade or the Royal Navy.

In the Caribbean

How Teach ended up as the pirate Blackbeard in the Caribbean is a mystery. He may have taken a job on board a ship in Bristol. Experts believe it is more likely he joined the Royal Navy. The navy was growing quickly and taking on many **recruits**.

A global war

Blackbeard's first naval experience probably came in the War of the Spanish **Succession** (1701–1714). The part of the war fought in North America between 1702 and 1713 was known as Queen Anne's War. The war began as a fight over who should become ruler of Spain. It grew into a fight between Spain and France on one side and Britain, Austria, and some states in what is now Germany on the other. Spain lost much of its territory when it was eventually defeated in 1714.

★★★ A TRADING CENTER

Bristol was the center of Britain's slave trade. Ships from the port took goods to West Africa. They carried slaves from Africa to the Caribbean, then more goods from the Caribbean back to Britain. The slave trade made Bristol the most important city in England after London.

French and English ships clash in October 1707 during the War of the Spanish Succession.

Recruits New members of the military services.

Succession Passing a position from one person to another.

In the Caribbean

The first time Edward Teach is mentioned in any records is as a crew member for the English pirate Benjamin Hornigold.

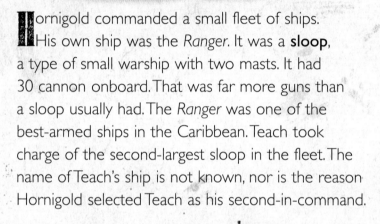

Hornigold commanded a small fleet of ships. His own ship was the *Ranger*. It was a **sloop**, a type of small warship with two masts. It had 30 cannon onboard. That was far more guns than a sloop usually had. The *Ranger* was one of the best-armed ships in the Caribbean. Teach took charge of the second-largest sloop in the fleet. The name of Teach's ship is not known, nor is the reason Hornigold selected Teach as his second-in-command.

Hornigold's ship *Ranger* was well armed. It was also fast enough to catch other ships.

Teach's crew loved stealing Madeira, a type of wine made in the Portuguese Madeira Islands.

Teach had to be able to maneuver his vessel during attacks on other ships. He also had to find his way through the islands of the Caribbean. It is likely that Teach was already a skilled sailor.

Life at sea

In 1717, Hornigold and Teach attacked Spanish and Portuguese ships throughout the Caribbean. They were careful not to attack British ships, however, so the British **authorities** did not try to stop them. The pirates stole cargo such as flour and wine. They later sold the goods at high prices.

Teach got a reputation for being tough and wild. He and his crew enjoyed drinking the liquor they stole. When they raided one ship in late September 1717, they only stole their favorite drink, Madeira wine. They sank the ship with the rest of its cargo still in the hold.

BENJAMIN HORNIGOLD

Benjamin Hornigold was one of the most successful pirates of what is often called the Golden Age of Piracy. He made a fortune from his piracy. Unlike Blackbeard, he also survived his time as a pirate. He was granted a **pardon** by the British. He later became a pirate hunter and died in a shipwreck in 1719.

Sloop A light, fast sailing ship.

Authorities People who enforce laws on behalf of a government.

Pardon Forgiveness for a crime.

Focus: Pirates and Privateers

Like Sir Walter Raleigh, Hornigold started his career as a privateer. The difference between pirates and privateers was not always clear.

Privateers were sailors who had permission from a monarch or government to attack and seize goods from the ships of other nations. This was a useful way for countries to be able to harm their enemy's trade.

In the 17th century, the English government encouraged privateers such as Sir Walter Raleigh to attack Spanish ships and settlements. However, privateers could make a lot of money and the English found it difficult to recruit ordinary sailors for the Royal Navy. In the 18th century the English stopped supporting privateers.

French privateers known as corsairs attack vessels in the Mediterranean. Privateers sailed in many of the world's seas.

Pirate or privateer?

After the War of the Spanish Succession ended in 1714, many privateers were no longer protected by their governments. Instead they were considered to be pirates. These pirates continued to raid enemy ships and take their goods, but they kept everything for themselves.

English and Dutch privateers and pirates were most successful in the Caribbean. They attacked Spanish **galleons** carrying gold and silver from Spain's American colonies back to Europe. A single cargo could be worth a fortune.

LETTERS OF MARQUE

A privateer carried a document known as a letter of marque. This was an official license from a government. It gave the bearer permission to attack enemy ships. It also said the privateer could keep or sell any goods that were seized during an attack.

This is a copy of a letter of marque issued by Britain's Queen Anne in 1703.

Galleons Large sailing ships, usually with three decks and three masts.

Becoming Blackbeard

Hornigold did not want to attack British ships. He feared that would risk a confrontation with the Royal Navy. Teach had no such worries.

Hornigold had a **policy** of only attacking Spanish, French, and Portuguese ships. Teach and many other members of Hornigold's crew did not agree. They wanted to be able to attack anyone. The War of the Spanish Succession was over. The sailors were now branded as pirates rather than privateers. They figured they would act like pirates. That meant attacking ships from any nation.

A growing reputation

In late 1717, Hornigold's men voted to attack any vessel, including British ships. Hornigold refused to accept their decision. He decided to head to Jamaica in his sloop, the *Ranger*. Most of his crew remained with Teach, who was the commander of one of

Hornigold's other ships, the *Revenge*. Teach and Hornigold never saw one another again.

Around this time, Teach began using the name Blackbeard. It was based on his appearance. The only known eyewitness account of Teach describes him as being "a tall **Spare** Man with a very black beard which he wore very long."

Jamaica was one of the centers of British power in the Caribbean. Hornigold headed there after he left Blackbeard.

A GENERAL HISTORY OF NOTORIOUS PYRATES

Most of what we know about Blackbeard and other famous pirates of the Caribbean comes from A General History of Notorious Pyrates. The book was published in Britain in 1724 by Captain Charles Johnson. Johnson's stories seem highly exaggerated. It is difficult to judge how accurate they are.

Policy A set of ideas that shapes the actions of an individual or a group.

Spare Without any excess fat.

A Captured Ship

Late in 1717, Edward Teach took command of a new ship. He renamed it the Queen Anne's Revenge.

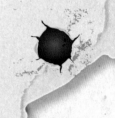

On November 28, 1717, Teach captured a huge French ship named *La Concord*. Experts are not sure whether he was on his own. Some experts think the *Concord* was captured before Benjamin Hornigold gave up piracy, and that Hornigold also took part in the attack. The French navy had used the *Concord* during the War of the Spanish Succession. In 1717, it was being used as a slave ship. The *Concord* was on a voyage to carry slaves from Africa to the Americas.

Most of the slaves from the Concord were abandoned on the Caribbean island of Bequia.

This is a computer reconstruction of the *Queen Anne's Revenge*, as Blackbeard renamed the *Concord*.

A NEW SHIP

For Blackbeard, the captured Concord was perfect. It was big and fast, with plenty of room for cannons. The pirate equipped it with 40 guns and renamed it Queen Anne's Revenge. He was now ready to control the Caribbean.

The pirates came alongside the *Concord*. They opened fire through their gun ports, killing some of *Concord*'s crew. The French captain surrendered. Blackbeard forced him to sail to the island of Bequia. Some of the slaves onboard may have joined the pirates. Others were left on Bequia. Blackbeard kept the *Concord* as his **flagship**. He gave the French crew a small ship to return home in.

Gun ports Openings in the sides of a ship that allow cannon to be fired through them.

Flagship The ship that carries the commander of a fleet.

17

Focus: Pirate Ships

For pirates, speed was the most important quality in a ship. They needed to be able to catch their victims and then make a fast escape.

The "Jolly Roger" was the most famous pirate flag.

The fastest type of ship was the sloop. It could overtake merchant ships carrying cargo. A sloop was usually about 60 feet (18 m) long. It carried at least 12 cannon. Most pirates sailed sloops made in Jamaica or Bermuda. The ships could sail and anchor in shallow water. This meant pirate ships could be hidden in sheltered bays without running aground.

Most pirates stole the ships they used. They looked out for sloops they could adapt, then added cannons, and removed cabins. That made more room for everyone to sleep, because pirate crews were bigger than regular ships' crews.

Blackbeard favored sloops, but he also liked larger vessels. He stole a two-masted brigantine named the *Sea Nymph*. It was big and slow, but Blackbeard wanted a large ship that reflected his status as a leading pirate.

Care of the ships

Pirates took care of their ships. They regularly cleaned off the **barnacles** that clung to the underside of the ship. This process was called careening. Keeping the vessels free from barnacles and thus more streamlined meant the ships could move more quickly through water. This made them faster than other ships.

THE JOLLY ROGER

All pirate ships flew a flag. A pirate flag was often called a "Jolly Roger." The flags varied, but they were usually painted with white skulls and crossed bones or crossed swords on a black background. The flag was intended to strike fear into the crews of other ships.

Workers build a ship in Jamaica. The island was well known for the quality of its shipbuilding.

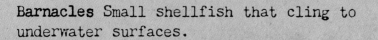

Barnacles Small shellfish that cling to underwater surfaces.

Terror on the Seas

After Hornigold decided to give up piracy in 1717, Blackbeard took command of his own pirate fleet.

A SHIP of War, of the third Rate With Rigging &c. at Anchor.

Section of a SHIP of War, of ye First Rate, shewing ye Inside.

This detailed plan shows a British warship. Such ships were heavy and slow. They were no match for the Queen Anne's Revenge.

Hornigold had taken the *Ranger* back to Jamaica. Blackbeard took command of the remaining ships and crew. He sailed in his flagship, the *Queen Anne's Revenge*. In December 1717, the pirates captured a British merchant ship named *Margaret*. It was the start of Blackbeard's campaign against ships in the Caribbean. News of Blackbeard's piracy spread in the British colonies of North America. Colonial Americans feared that he might attack their ports.

There was a story that Blackbeard put smoking fuses in his hair to make himself look more frightening. No one knows if this is true.

Growing stronger

The Royal Navy sent HMS *Scarborough* to look for Blackbeard. However, the *Queen Anne's Revenge* was too fast and well-armed for the naval ship. Instead, the British tried offering a pardon to the pirates. Blackbeard and most of his crew ignored the offer.

In March 1718, Blackbeard sailed to Central America. He recruited more men to his band of pirates. By April, he had five more vessels in his **flotilla**. Blackbeard began to think about targets in North America.

A SCARY APPEARANCE

As more stories about Blackbeard spread, descriptions of his appearance became more frightening. Some people claimed he fixed smoking fuses under his hat brim. Fuses were short pieces of rope used to fire cannons. Blackbeard was also said to carry many pistols.

Blockade of Charleston

Colonial Americans in Charleston, South Carolina, were frightened by stories about Blackbeard. In May 1718, their fears became reality.

Charleston Harbor was one of the most important ports in Britain's American colonies.

Blackbeard positioned his flotilla across the entrance to Charleston Harbor. The pirates stopped all other ships from entering or leaving the harbor. They stole the cargoes of other ships and imprisoned their crews.

Offering an exchange

At the time, the people of Charleston were busy fighting Native Americans who threatened the settlement. They had no spare resources to break the **blockade**. When Blackbeard captured a ship carrying some of Charleston's most important citizens, he offered a deal. He would free his prisoners and leave Charleston in exchange for medicine that he needed. If he did not get the medicine, he would cut off the heads of the prisoners.

However, when Blackbeard's pirates went to collect the medicine, they got so drunk that they nearly forgot to take it back to the ship. They finally remembered their mission. Blackbeard kept his word. He freed his prisoners and left Charleston.

CHARLESTON

Charleston was a good port for Blackbeard to attack. Both Spain and England said they owned it, but neither had military forces there. The town was under almost constant Native American attack. The inhabitants were so busy defending the port they could not also fight the pirates.

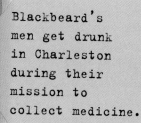

Blackbeard's men get drunk in Charleston during their mission to collect medicine.

Blockade The act of sealing off a place to prevent goods or people entering or leaving.

Run Aground!

After Blackbeard left Charleston in May 1718, he learned that the Royal Navy was sailing toward the Caribbean to rid it of pirates for good.

This house in North Carolina is one of a number of houses Blackbeard is said to have stayed in during 1717 and 1718.

Blackbeard headed north along the American coast. He sailed into Beaufort Inlet in what is now North Carolina. However, the *Queen Anne's Revenge* ran aground on a **sandbar**. It was badly damaged. Another of his ships also ran aground. Blackbeard decided to abandon both of the damaged ships.

Blackbeard had lost his best ship. He decided to accept a royal pardon. However, the previous pardon had only been offered for acts of piracy committed before January 5, 1718.

Stede Bonnet received his pardon in May 1718 but returned to piracy.

Bonnet is pardoned

Blackbeard had committed many crimes since January 1718. He was not sure if he would be given a pardon. He wanted to see what would happen if he asked for one. To find out without risking his own freedom, Blackbeard sent his second-in-command, Stede Bonnet, to ask the governor of North Carolina. The governor pardoned Bonnet. However, when Bonnet arrived back at Beaufort Inlet with the news, he found Blackbeard had gone. Only Bonnet's own ship remained. Despite receiving his pardon, Bonnet returned to piracy in July 1718.

STEDE BONNET

Bonnet was an unusual pirate. He came from a wealthy English family in Barbados. Known as the "gentleman-pirate," he was said to have joined Blackbeard to escape a disastrous marriage. After his pardon Bonnet soon returned to piracy. He was caught and hanged in December 1718.

Sandbar A long narrow bank of sand that is hidden underwater, often near the entrance to a river.

Blackbeard's Base

In June 1718, Blackbeard was finally given a pardon. He seemed willing to give up his life of crime.

After hearing that Bonnet had been given a pardon, Blackbeard applied for a pardon of his own. It was granted by Governor Charles Eden of North Carolina. Blackbeard spent the summer of 1718 near Bath, North Carolina. He moored his sloop off Ocracoke Island, where he made a base. His crew went to live in different settlements along the coast.

King Philip V of Spain began the War of the Quadruple Alliance to try to seize the French throne.

Back in action

Blackbeard's retirement from piracy did not last long. King Philip V of Spain declared war on France, which made **alliances** with Britain and other countries. The conflict was Blackbeard's chance to return to the seas not as a pirate but as a privateer, sailing on behalf of Britain.

Blackbeard sailed from Bath in one of his sloops, the *Adventure*. But he never became a privateer. Instead, he chose to become a pirate again. He sailed north along the North American coast, attacking any ships he found. In one attack, he seized a French ship and took it back to Ocracoke. He told Governor Eden he had found the ship abandoned at sea. He shared the ship's cargo with Eden and his government officials.

A PIRATE ALLY?

Many pirates operated along the North Carolina coast. The authorities did not try to stop them. Many people believed Governor Eden cooperated with the pirates and took some of their profits in return for leaving them alone.

Blackbeard's crew enjoy a feast at their base on Ocracoke Island.

Alliances Formal relationships between countries to achieve a particular goal.

A Popular Spot

Blackbeard was not the only pirate operating off the North American coast. Piracy was big business.

Charles Vane had one of the longest careers of any pirate. He sailed the Caribbean from 1716 to 1719.

Ocracoke Island was Blackbeard's favorite hiding place on the North American coast. It came within the **jurisdiction** of the governor of North Carolina. Some people said Governor Charles Eden deliberately helped the pirate.

Pirate visitors

One day in September 1718, Blackbeard was keeping watch on passing ships from his **mooring** on Ocracoke Island. He saw another ship approach. It belonged to an English pirate named Charles Vane. Vane had rejected the chance to be pardoned in July 1718 and was on the run from Blackbeard's old captain, Benjamin Hornigold, who had become a pirate hunter. Vane stayed on Ocracoke with Blackbeard. The island was also popular with "Calico Jack" and other pirates.

Borrowed time

But time was running out for Blackbeard. Governor Alexander Spotswood of Virginia was horrified at what was happening in neighboring North Carolina. Governors in other colonies were also worried. The pirates seemed to control the seas. North Carolina citizens who thought Governor Eden was working with Blackbeard asked Spotswood to act on their behalf and catch Blackbeard.

PIRATE HUNTERS

The British hired many pirate hunters. Some were former pirates, like Benjamin Hornigold. Others were private citizens, like William Rhett, a plantation owner. Rhett captured Stede Bonnet in 1718. Other pirate hunters were sailors in the Royal Navy.

Jurisdiction The territory or area in which an official or court has power to act.

Mooring A place where a boat or ship is tied up.

Focus: Pirate Life

A pirate's life was hard work. Even though they were outlaws, pirates lived by **a strict code of discipline.**

Pirates divide up the goods they have captured from a ship. Everyone was given an equal share.

Apirate crew normally numbered around 80 men. A pirate ship was cramped, so it had to be well run. The captain was in charge. His second-in-command was the quartermaster. He had an important job. The quartermaster was responsible for enforcing discipline. This could be difficult with a crew of tough outlaws. However, unlike on naval or merchant ships, pirate ships were **democratic**. The quartermaster was elected by the crew. The captain had the final word when the ship was chasing or being chased. The rest of the time all crew members had a say in how the ship was run.

Life on board

The pirates shared sleeping quarters. There were no special cabins for the captain or quartermaster. Pirates carried out everyday jobs, such as sharpening swords, mending sails, and keeping watch. There were long periods when pirates had nothing to do except play cards, gamble, and drink.

If a pirate broke the rules, punishments included **flogging** or having an ear cut off. For a serious crime, such as murder, the pirate was left on an island with just a pistol and some water. He soon died unless he was rescued.

SHIP'S ARTICLES

Every pirate had to sign the "ship's articles." The articles were a list of rules that had to be obeyed. If a pirate could not write, he signed with a mark like an X.

Pirates board a ship to fight its crew. Most pirates fought with swords and pistols.

Democratic Relating to a system in which everyone has a say in decisions.

Flogging A beating with a whip as a punishment.

The Governor's Decision

Governor Alexander Spotswood of Virginia decided that he had to take action against Blackbeard.

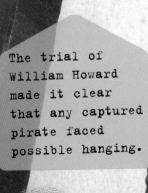

Between voyages, some of Blackbeard's pirates lived in ports along the Virginia coast. They included the quartermaster, William Howard. Governor Spotswood of Virginia ordered Howard's arrest.

Howard was put on trial. Governor Eden of North Carolina was sympathetic to pirates. He hired lawyers to represent Howard. The lawyers argued that Governor Spotswood had no power to arrest Howard because there had not been any piracy in Virginia. Spotswood argued that piracy was generally out of control and so it was indeed a problem for Virginia. Howard was found guilty and sentenced to death. He was spared after a pardon was sent from London.

The trial of William Howard made it clear that any captured pirate faced possible hanging.

Useful information

Before he was ordered to pardon Howard, however, Spotswood made the pirate reveal Blackbeard's hiding place.

Risk of capture was increasing for Blackbeard. The Howard case showed that a pirate could be arrested anywhere. In November 1718, a Royal **Proclamation** offered a huge reward for information leading to Blackbeard's capture or death. The Assembly of Virginia also offered a reward for Blackbeard's capture. Spotswood hired Royal Navy Lieutenant Robert Maynard to lead a mission to find the pirate.

Many people criticized the mansion Spotswood built in Richmond. They said it was too extravagant.

ALEXANDER SPOTSWOOD

Alexander Spotswood served as Lieutenant Governor of Virginia from 1710 to 1722. He helped to increase the colony and encouraged settlers to move inland from the coast. He also made a peace treaty with the local Iroquois people. Spotswood built the new Governor's Mansion in Richmond.

Proclamation An official announcement about an important subject.

Focus: Pirates and the Law

One reason Blackbeard and other pirates operated in North America was that the British were targeting pirates in the Caribbean.

Pirates declared Nassau in the Bahamas to be a "pirate republic." The many pirates who used the port included Blackbeard.

The financial rewards from piracy were much higher than a sailor could earn in the Royal Navy or on a merchant ship. For the British and their colonial officials in the Caribbean and North America, the question was how to make piracy seem less attractive.

Granting pardons

One way to stop piracy was to grant pardons to pirates. King George I issued a royal pardon to all pirates at the start of 1718. Later that year, Woodes Rogers arrived in the Bahamas. He was the first

Royal Governor of the Bahamas. The islands were a base for many pirates in the Caribbean. One of Rogers' first tasks was to stop the pirates. Rogers convinced many pirates to accept pardons and give up piracy. He forbade others from using the Bahamas as a base.

Pirate hunters

Woodes Rogers had been a privateer. He understood the pirates. The British often **enlisted** former pirates and privateers to hunt pirates down. Former pirates, such as Benjamin Hornigold, had the advantage of knowing where pirates liked to sail and moor.

THE BAHAMAS

In the two decades after 1700, the Bahamas became a pirates' paradise. The islands had no government, so pirates had little chance of being caught. Around 200 pirates and hundreds of fugitives from nearby Spanish colonies lived there before Rogers imposed law and order.

This painting from 1729 marks the success of Woodes Rogers (right) who finally rid the Bahamas of pirates.

Enlist To recruit someone to join the armed services.

Maynard's Mission

Governor Spotswood gave Lieutenant
Robert Maynard the task of capturing
Blackbeard, dead or alive.

Maynard found
Blackbeard at
the pirate's
favorite hideout,
on Ocracoke
Island, North
Carolina.

On November 17, 1718, Maynard took command of two ships named *Jane* and *Ranger*. With a total of nearly 60 men, he set sail to hunt down Blackbeard. The pirate William Howard had already given Governor Spotswood information about where Blackbeard was hiding. Four days later, on November 21, Maynard found Blackbeard and his crew anchored off Ocracoke Island.

Maynard takes position

Maynard had the advantage. Blackbeard had only one sloop and around 25 men. Maynard positioned his ships so that no boat could enter or leave the inlet. Meanwhile, Blackbeard had no idea his hiding place had been discovered. He spent the evening ashore on Ocracoke Island. He had dinner with some friends.

The next morning, Maynard spotted Blackbeard, who was back onboard his ship the *Adventure*. Maynard prepared to attack. Blackbeard had realized that Maynard's ships were blocking his escape. The pirate wanted to find out who his enemy was, and started to **taunt** Maynard. He tried to provoke him into battle.

Ocracoke is formed out of sand dunes. It was largely uninhabited until 1750.

BLACKBEARD'S TAUNTS

An eyewitness noted the verbal exchange between the pirate and Maynard. Blackbeard yelled, "Villains, who are you? And from whence came you?" Maynard replied, "You may see by our Colors we are no Pyrates." Blackbeard raised his glass to Maynard, saying, "Seize my Soul if I give you Quarters, or take any from you." Maynard replied that he did not intend to show any quarter, or mercy.

Taunt To provoke someone to do something by using insulting remarks.

Last Battle

Although he was greatly outnumbered, Blackbeard was not going to surrender to Maynard without a fight.

Most of Blackbeard's crew were ashore on the mainland. Only about 25 men remained on the *Adventure*. As Maynard's ships, *Ranger* and *Jane*, sailed toward the *Adventure*, Blackbeard turned his ship so that his gun ports were in position to open fire on them.

Fighting begins

It is not known who started firing first, but the fight was devastating. Maynard lost around one-third of his men as cannonballs rained down on his ships. Meanwhile, Maynard's cannon fire cut the jib sheet on the *Adventure*. The jib sheet is a rope that controls the **jib**, which helps to steer a ship. With the jib sheet cut, Blackbeard's crew could no longer control the direction or speed of the ship. The *Adventure* ran aground on a sandbar.

Blackbeard turned the *Adventure* so all its cannon were facing Maynard's vessels.

The *Ranger* (left) crashes into the *Adventure* in this drawing of the naval clash.

Maynard's attack

Maynard maneuvered his damaged ships toward Blackbeard's grounded vessel. The ships came within touching distance. Unknown to Blackbeard, Maynard had ordered the men on the *Ranger* to hide belowdecks. The trick would prove decisive in the battle.

As the *Ranger* approached the *Adventure*, it appeared to be empty. Blackbeard thought the crew had all been killed. He gave the order to board the ship. As Blackbeard's pirates leaped from the *Adventure* to the *Ranger*, they were unprepared for what happened next.

ROBERT MAYNARD

Robert Maynard served in the Royal Navy. Little is known about his early career, but he was made a lieutenant in 1707. He was promoted to captain later in his career in 1740. Maynard died in 1751 and was buried in Kent, in southeast England. He is best remembered as being the man who caught and killed Blackbeard, the notorious pirate.

Jib A triangular sail set in front of the forward mast on a sailing ship.

Death of Blackbeard

As the two ships came together, it was clear the battle would be a fight to the death.

The pirates had thrown **grenades** onto the *Ranger* as they boarded it. When the smoke from the grenades cleared, the pirates were shocked to find Maynard's men on deck. Soon, the men were fighting hand-to-hand with guns and swords. The deck was already slippery with blood from Blackbeard's **broadside** attack.

Blackbeard (left) and Maynard fight on the deck of the Ranger.

Blackbeard struck

Blackbeard and Maynard moved toward each other. Maynard wounded Blackbeard with a shot from his pistol. Both men drew their swords, but Blackbeard's cutlass snapped Maynard's sword. The pirate was ready to strike Maynard when one of Maynard's men slashed Blackbeard's neck with his sword.

Blackbeard fought on but loss of blood weakened him. Maynard's men shot at him and continued to slash at him with their cutlasses. Eventually Blackbeard collapsed. He was dead. Maynard later claimed that Blackbeard had suffered at least 25 wounds: 5 gunshot wounds and at least 20 sword slashes.

When Blackbeard's men realized their leader was dead, they surrendered. The pirate's reign of terror was over. Maynard beheaded Blackbeard and threw his body into the Atlantic Ocean.

OFF WITH HIS HEAD!

Maynard put the pirate's head at the front of his ship as proof that Blackbeard was dead. This was the evidence Maynard needed to collect rewards from Britain and Virginia for the pirate's capture or death.

Maynard put Blackbeard's head on the spit at the front of his ship. The head was later put on a stake in the Hampton River in Virginia as a warning to other would-be pirates.

Grenades Small bombs that are thrown by hand.

Broadside The firing of all guns on one side of a warship.

Focus: Blackbeard's Legacy

Blackbeard is the most famous pirate of all time, even though he was far from being the most successful.

Blackbeard terrorized the Caribbean and North America during the so-called "Golden Age of Piracy." This was a period that began in around 1670. Blackbeard's death in 1718 marked the end of the pirate era.

Blackbeard's historical **reputation** was created by Charles Johnson's 1724 book, *A General History of Notorious Pyrates*. Johnson described how ruthless Blackbeard was. But there are so many stories about Blackbeard that it is impossible to know what is true and what has been made up.

Books and movies

Of all the pirates operating in the Caribbean, Blackbeard was among the most notorious. That is why he caught the public imagination. Two of the most famous pirates in literature were based on Blackbeard: Long John Silver from *Treasure Island* by

Robert Louis Stevenson (1883) and Captain Hook from *Peter Pan* by J. M. Barrie (1904).

Blackbeard has also been represented in movies since the earliest Hollywood films. Most recently Blackbeard was the model for Captain Jack Sparrow in the *Pirates of the Caribbean* movies. Johnny Depp, who plays Jack Sparrow, was made to look like old illustrations of Blackbeard.

Johnny Depp (center) plays Captain Jack Sparrow in the movie series, Pirates of the Caribbean, which began in 2003.

QUEEN ANNE'S REVENGE

In 1996 archeologists found a shipwreck off the coast of North Carolina. Experts believe the wreck is Blackbeard's ship, Queen Anne's Revenge. They have excavated the underwater site. Among other finds, they have retrieved 31 cannons.

Reputation How someone or something is judged by other people.

ROGUES' GALLERY

Blackbeard was not the only pirate sailing the high seas. There were many other colorful characters, including women pirates.

Anne Bonny
(c.1700–c.1782)

Anne Bonny was an Irishwoman who became a famous pirate. She began her career as an outlaw on the sloop commanded by her boyfriend and later husband, "Calico Jack." She fought alongside the other pirates and was captured with her husband in 1720. She was found guilty but spared from hanging because she was going to have a child. She died in jail.

"Calico Jack"
(1682–1720)

Jack's real name was John Rackham. He was a British pirate who sailed from the Bahamas and Cuba. He is best known for designing the "Jolly Roger," a pirate flag with a skull and two crossed bones or crossed swords. He had two women in his crew, including his wife, Anne Bonny. Jack's nickname came from the calico cloth clothes he wore. He was hanged in 1720.

William Kidd
(c.1645–1701)

Captain William Kidd was a Scottish sailor who operated in the Indian Ocean. Kidd said he was a privateer, but many people saw him as a pirate. He was caught and hanged for murdering one of his own crew. Kidd was said to have buried a vast treasure somewhere on the coast of North America.

Mary Read
(c.1690–1721)

Mary Read was an English pirate who dressed as a man. She was a member of the "Calico Jack" crew. Read was captured and imprisoned with "Calico Jack" and Anne Bonny. But like Bonny, she was spared execution. Read also died in jail.

Charles Vane
(c.1680–1721)

Charles Vane was another English pirate who operated during the "Golden Age of Piracy." He was based in the lawless Bahamas until he was finally captured and executed after a long career in piracy. Vane was known for his cruelty toward those he attacked.

GLOSSARY

Alliances Formal relationships between countries to achieve a particular goal.

Authorities People who enforce laws on behalf of a government.

Barnacles Small shellfish that cling to underwater surfaces.

Blockade The act of sealing off a place to prevent goods or people entering or leaving.

Broadside The firing of all guns on one side of a warship.

Colony An area under the control of another country.

Democratic Relating to a system in which everyone has a say in decisions.

Enlist To recruit someone to join the armed services.

Flagship The ship that carries the commander of a fleet.

Flogging A beating with a whip as a punishment.

Flotilla A small fleet of ships.

Galleons Large sailing ships, usually with three decks and three masts.

Grenades Small bombs that are thrown by hand.

Gun ports Openings in the sides of a ship that allow cannon to be fired.

Jib A triangular sail set in front of the forward mast on a sailing ship.

Jurisdiction The territory in which an official or court has power to act.

Merchant ships: Ships that carry cargo or passengers.

Mooring A place where a boat or ship is tied up.

Pardon Forgiveness for a crime.

Policy A set of ideas that shapes the actions of an individual or a group.

Privateers: Sailors with official permission to raid ships from other countries.

Proclamation An official announcement about an important subject.

Recruits New members of the military services.

Reputation How someone or something is judged by other people.

Sandbar A long narrow bank of sand that is hidden underwater, often near the entrance of a river.

Sloop A light, fast sailing ship.

Spare Without any excess fat.

Succession Passing a position from one person to another.

Taunt To provoke someone to do something by using insulting remarks.

FURTHER RESOURCES

Books

Brew, Jim. *Pirates*. Torque Books: History's Greatest Warriors. Minneapolis, MN: Bellwether Media, 2012.

Croce, Pat. *Blackbeard*. Philadelphia, PA: Running Press Kids, 2011.

Gagne, Tammy. *Blackbeard (Edward Teach)*. Pirates Around the World: Terror on the High Seas. Hockessin, DL: Mitchell Lane Publishers, 2015.

Hamilton, Sue. *Blackbeard*. Pirates! Edina, MN: ABDO Publishing Company, 2007.

Jenson-Elliott, Cindy. *The Most Famous Pirates*. Pirates! Mankato, MN: Capstone Press, 2012.

Weintraub, Aileen. *Blackbeard: Eighteenth-Century Pirate of the Spanish Main and Carolina Coasts*. New York: PowerKids Press, 2005.

Websites

http://www.nationalgeographic.com/pirates/bbeard.html
A page about Blackbeard for kids from National Geographic, with links to pages about pirate life.

http://www.qaronline.org/History/StoryofBlackbeard.aspx
A biography of Blackbeard from the website dedicated to restoring the *Queen Anne's Revenge*, the pirate's famous flagship in North Carolina.

http://ncpedia.org/biography/blackbeard-the-pirate
An entry on Blackbeard from the NCpedia, an encyclopedia of North Carolina.

http://www.thepirateking.com/bios/teach_edward.htm
A biography of Blackbeard from a privately maintained website dedicated to history's famous pirates and their lives.

Publisher's note to educators and parents: Our editors have carefully reviewed these websites to ensure that they are suitable for students. Many websites change frequently, however, and we cannot guarantee that a site's future contents will continue to meet our high standards of quality and educational value. Be advised that students should be closely supervised whenever they access the Internet.

INDEX